Honesty

by Kelli L. Hicks

Content Consultants:
Melissa Z. Pierce, L.C.S.W.
Sam Williams, M.Ed.

Educational Media

rourkeeducationalmedia.com

Teacher Notes available at
rem4teachers.com

www.rourkeeducationalmedia.com

Melissa Z. Pierce is a licensed clinical social worker with a background in counseling in the home and school group settings. Melissa is currently a life coach. She brings her experience as a L.C.S.W. and parent to the *Little World Social Skills* collection and the *Social Skills and More* program.

Sam Williams has a master's degree in education. Sam Williams is a former teacher with over 10 years of classroom experience. He has been a literacy coach, professional development writer and trainer, and is a published author. He brings his experience in child development and classroom management to this series.

PHOTO CREDITS: Cover: © Sean Locke; page 3: © Nicole S. Young; page 5: © digitalskillet; page 6: © Wuka; page 7: © Dejan Ristovski; page 9: © Doug Berry; page 11: © Dmitriy Shironosov; page 13: © Rmarmion; page 15: © Joshua Hodge Photography; page 17: © Chris Bernard; page 19: © kristian sekulic; page 21: © Agnieszka Kirinicjanow

Illustrations by: Anita DuFalla

Edited by: Precious McKenzie

Cover and Interior designed by: Tara Raymo

Library of Congress EPCN Data

Honesty / Kelli L. Hicks
(Little World Social Skills)
ISBN 978-1-61810-132-7 (hard cover)(alk. paper)
ISBN 978-1-61810-265-2 (soft cover)
Library of Congress Control Number: 2011945276

Rourke Educational Media
Printed in the United States of America,
North Mankato, Minnesota

rourkeeducationalmedia.com

customerservice@rourkeeducationalmedia.com • PO Box 643328 Vero Beach, Florida 32964

What do you say if your mom asks, "Did you eat a cookie before dinner?" And, the **truth** is that you did.

Would you **answer** with honesty? When you are **honest**, you tell the truth, no matter what happens.

He ate the cookie.

5

If you spill juice on the floor and it splashes into a big **puddle**, tell a grownup you did it. Then help clean up the mess.

When you are at school do your own work, even if you make a **mistake**. Everybody makes mistakes.

When you find something that doesn't belong to you, don't keep it. Be honest and try to find out who lost it.

Sometimes it is hard to be honest. It can be scary to tell the truth. Nobody wants to get into trouble.

Telling the truth makes others **proud** of you. It tells them that you can be trusted.

Honesty Quiz

Are you honest? Answer these questions to find out.

1. Do you always tell the truth? ⬭ yes ⬭ no

2. If you find something that is not yours, do you give it back? ⬭ yes ⬭ no

3. Do you do your own work? ⬭ yes ⬭ no

4. Do others trust you to make a good choice? ⬭ yes ⬭ no

5. Do you clean up your own mess? ⬭ yes ⬭ no

It takes strength and courage to be honest but you can do it!

Being honest makes you feel good about you!

Picture Glossary

answer (AN-sur):
When you say something to reply to someone else or a solution to a problem.

honest (ON-ist):
A quality of someone who does not lie, steal, or cheat.

mistake (muh-STAKE):
When you have a misunderstanding or when you mess up.

proud (PROUD):
When you are pleased or happy with something that you or someone else has done.

puddle (PUHD-uhl):
A small pool of water or some other liquid.

truth (TROOTH):
When you tell all the real facts.

Index

Websites

www.k12.hi.us/~mkunimit/honesty.htm
www.tellitagan.com/
www.storiestogrowby.com/choose.php

About the Author

Kelli L. Hicks is honestly a homebody who loves her children, Mack and Bear, her husband, and her golden retriever, Gingerbread. She is honest when she gets caught eating cookies before dinner.

Ask The Author!
www.rem4students.com